Our World

Our World

Poems

Shelby Stephenson

Press 53
Winston-Salem

Press 53, LLC
PO Box 30314
Winston-Salem, NC 27130

First Edition

Copyright © 2018 by Shelby Stephenson

All rights reserved, including the right of reproduction in whole or in part in any form except in the case of brief quotations embodied in critical articles or reviews. For permission, contact publisher at editor@Press53.com, or at the address above.

Cover design and cover art,
Copyright © 2018 by Jacob Stephenson,
used by permission of the artist.

Author photo by Jeff Davis

Library of Congress Control Number
2018935976

Printed on acid-free paper
ISBN 978-1-941209-79-0

to Nin

and to Fred and Susan Chappell

Some parts of *Our World* have appeared, sometimes in different form, in the following publications:

The Barefoot Review: "Mood: Forever a Sequel"

Jellyfish Whispers: "Across the Wide Missouri"

Intimacy (Anthology): "More"

North State Journal: "Life Renewed," "Songbirds," "Walk Into Spring"

Otis Nebula Magazine: "Duo"

Parting Gifts: "Mushrooms, My Love, Could Send Us," in chapbook, *Play My Music Anyhow*

Pembroke Magazine: "Of a Time," "Quiet Snow"

The Torch: "Our World"

Contents

I

Our World	3
Sweet Song	4
Mushrooms, My Love, Could Send Us	5
A Certain One Among Many	6
Lovework	7
Now, Voyager	8
Shadowlines	9
End of Day	10
Twirling Detail	11
Lost Heart	12
Across the Wide Missouri	13
Of a Time	14
Crying Holy to Pay Chastity's Rent	15
Open Books	16
Separation	17
A Plea Against Worry	18
The Telephone Gown	19
For Your Eyes	20
Look at Us	21

II

Duo	25
Mood: Forever a Sequel	26
More	29
Love Clouds	30
Quiet Snow	31
Decades of Prayer	34
Empty Shelves Song	36
Signs of Spring	37
Our Unspoken Love	40
Moonlight	41
Always There	44
The Old Well	46
Love Song	48

Gentle Kisses	49
Night and Day	50
Wind-Face	52
Crashing Waves	53
Under Derek's Awning	54
Your Head Pillowed	55
For Nin	56

III

Walk into Spring	59
Life Renewed	60
Clothes	61
Flight	64
The Warmth of the Fire	65
Searching	66
Love Remembered	67
The Mother's Tale	69
Flowers in the Snow	70
Drizzle	73
Storms Never Last	74
Note to Diana	75
Stash	76
Lament	78
Dearest	79
Little Farm Dogs	80
Songbirds	82
Poem	83
Countering Terminus	84
Slips in the Night	86
Running Toward Your Hair	87
Flummoxed & Bumfuzzled	88
Anxiety	89
Author Biography	91

I

OUR WORLD

If today the sun should set and clothe me
From top to bottom and free up certain
Perfect, hard unknowns to lead footsteps you
And I trace for all to see our troubles,

Should we shower shine as the simple joy
I feel from being close to you in rhyme,
As you sway kitchen's clattering foil
To wrap a piece of rindy-kicking lime?

And as you hand a drink to me, my hand
Outreaching, touching yours, surely you know
The sense our world's weather cannot contain
That deep and wide gladness Eternity
Places blisses surrounding where we go—
Is our harmony all without a stance?

SWEET SONG

Your face comes to me in a parlor
game to name a year-end dance.
I waltz across states and years without
you and with you, too: you keep coming
back to me; I lean down to kiss your face.
We embrace the way two, just-married, do.
Your hair's a swish on either side where motion
curls. I am at a loss to say how all *this* could be.

MUSHROOMS, MY LOVE, COULD SEND US

among spores
pulling
and
weeding
needing
umbrella-shapes
agrarian fungi
edible
as
sprung
proverbs
pulpy
gerunds
gather
to
flatten
folds
in
boring
hushes

A CERTAIN ONE AMONG MANY

On this quiet hill atop Pleasant Grove,
My township here, countenances appear
As bees clover hovering on white tops.
I share your images, unlocked inside
My heart, promises, some waltzes, motions
Savoring Paul's Hill: the music picks up:
That Texas Playboy, Wills, scats a holler—
San Antonio RO-O-ose—I gain
My tone-tunes in pitches senses scramble.

LOVEWORK

Country music I do love: still
I think of one I lost and found,
Lose, find—she's up and down a hill
As now; yet she'll come around,
Always does: then I shall delve
Into her charms, farmboy I am—
> *I lean myself into the helve*
> *And hoe the row I've got to hoe.*

Poetry and songs seldom sin.
Abandon Impresario?
I swirl for holes, plant slips to shelve
In small chaps, holding on—tiptoe—
> *I lean myself into the helve*
> *And hoe the row I've got to hoe.*

NOW, VOYAGER

What if our "untold want"
Did find us sailing forth
Among the stars all blent,
And no moon yet in orb.

I never asked you—leave
Me lonely and go on,
Set your way untaken.
I took what road found me.

You remind me—that line
About—why do we need
The moon—we've got the stars:
Let's seek those paths the child
Courted—lamb, night, the lion.

SHADOWLINES

So fare thee well, lovely lass, fifty years,
A winter's cup running on in arrears,
Up-to-date the history of our race
The sun provideth and takes to that place
He is climbing as Rood the Warrior
So bold we are free to read the story.

I was groomed in Leda's silence so long
The words which might bloom flowers on this hill,
On a crest of stone, where I am and know
The pipping muscle hardens, tune no thrill
While cherries clutch chicks in The Riddle Song,
Plus no bone soon in sight, though, there it is—
The baby, the story, known, no crying.
Your body in mine shades effects of time.

END OF DAY

What if the world fell into a swirl, you not here
except in my mind, the sunset an egg on my face to renew
poses? Several apply to my case, shaping decades of absences
and hollowing out silences. The child of the lion's limbs,
the lamb lying by, plus the dove feeding among
the musings the sunflowers yellow the first hunting day.

TWIRLING DETAIL

Listen, Nin,
For Depression's bottom-line.
It clouts my heart's thrashing shore.
I surf waves above—below,
While you twirl at a Post-it during the day.
Clouds gray the grocery list.
Night eyes spheres over Paul's Hill.

LOST HEART

Will you remember all the misery
Which we raked up and bagged as usury,
Squirming scruffing, snuffling slovenly lost,
The clothes we wore, misplaced, our body's cost;
Mine you drew like a rope on a pulley
All wavering inside of me—missiles.

Recall the loose talk? That burden? O yes,
There are "they"; like ghosts, their tongues never rest;
Reveries cannot cancel sterling Truth
Or waltzing regret's close and swelling ruse,
With steps, timed, the dancing slow—a sidle—
Toward parting, wedging the heart's recital.

ACROSS THE WIDE MISSOURI

Since you drifted away, taking your heart
And leaving me with your wavelets as part
Of longing to be with you, I shall go
Now, for we know life's not art, but the slow,
High way of reconciliation, one
Space between separation's craving bone
And the wishful, thinking, chill-healing drive
To want to see myself without the bride
These words do fail to page, praying softly
As dreams break and curve in floods arias
River into your voice I give away,
Seeing your face rescued in every wave
The past distributes ghostly ways to graves.

OF A TIME

Those years are gone forever, Sweet,
Socked, soaked, gone for ever!
      We look in glass—
      Nothing comes back;
But the hands fumbling, buttery, a path,
      To stifle Love's blunt quiver.

The road we opened up nearby,
Shoulders, littered debris;
      But we yet yearn,
      Lean toward return,
Like ghosts miming times we shared, memories,
Hopes and tears, one big, veiled sea,
      To vent Love's skimming spray.

CRYING HOLY TO PAY CHASTITY'S RENT

O I did not do it: cut down the tree,
My Love. Paradise stores slips in your mind.
The vows years ago set us tarrying,
Entranced on Romance's constant which ground
Our bodies to tenders already formed
To bring your baritone ukulele
Strumming through our golden years. The kettle's
Drum, a midnight moon on the beach, keep time.
Stay here and watch the Sun rise all around,
You say, for Love's sake, I suppose, and hope
That draws us into our memories, too,
Mothers, fathers, family, Phantasies.

OPEN BOOKS

You and I are open books, my love.
I am your center-fold of syllables
Trying to find what I don't know.
Your instinct carries your way,
A quick-read, a room aching full of heart.
You send me exactnesses—
Breaths and stresses—lovely hugs
And words beyond eyes of any sages.

SEPARATION

I am not a fool for still loving you,
        Clambering down from your big four-poster
To love's surrounding visions of blue,
        Sunrise on the beach, seawater's yodel
Rounding up the happiness you flower—
        Our hope for normal mood to continue,
While days undress hours and sack one bower
        We might seek to surrender—remember
The love we wear in waves of worn
Closeness in places—so hot—we shower—
        Melding exigencies scattering reaps.
We spoon, against your warm back, I, my face—
        My eyes, your hair, sweets.
Your rituals mourn our love at your pace.

A PLEA AGAINST WORRY

Your worries shrink up and fuse my feelings
With you, your instinct already the tears
You shed from being jerked into dealings
You consider the bane of love's seasons.

Consider not giving up ground to pain.
Do not play with fire and burn your fingers.
What's best for you, my love? Please do not lean
Toward any thought which erupts into shame.

What shapes like a drama on a tear.
The forms become a waiting room for Main,
Unholy ghosts' gestures bring utterly
From other sides of imperfection there;
Yet, my love, can more encompassing be
Our oneness, rare, plus your instinct in me?

THE TELEPHONE GOWN

What dress society calls on you to wear!
The world's one veil flies aloof now to moan
Alone how sad Fate wipes your smiling tears,
As I love to see how the gown, you groaned,
You washed with your telephone book, fought Fear,
To fade with your wear: "What was pink is stone,"
You sighed, then fluffed and shushed the fluty sleeves
Which course your arms flailing from your tall bed
You climb down from. Your feet flower the floor.
Your top stops to show your elbows (well said),
Your polka-dot suit, too, I adore—peace
Your heart sacrifices. The past lies Dead
For spring; the meadowlark sings at ease
And the grass, laughing, wafts waves and spreads.

FOR YOUR EYES

I would not arrange the words if I could
      Upon a page for troubadours to sing.
Toward fame's misbelieving neon I would
      Moon June's syllables—spoon my love to ring
Gold's success as a hillbilly singer.
      Just let me remember your eyes in sleep.
They spread your child's shyness like a ringer
      Of church-bells might hold back the meddling deep
Echoes circling heads of lovers mourning
      To kiss each other's eyes, open their worlds
To sights divine as angels adorning
      Smiles with envy at yours, their matter,
      Your instinct teeming with sight on latter
Thoughts darkness works to lift light from your world.

LOOK AT US

If, my Sweet, by words our Love be contained,
        Please know that I carry you in my heart;
Syllables you allow my hand to pen
Shall warm my Muse, since you are unconstrained,
        O, over and over, doing your part
As much for me, yourself, as we—to win
The notion that two—look at us—since we
Cannot harm our world's view, as it gains
        Perspective, looking in: picture how smart
Children appear in windows our hearts see,
Our lives filled with love—peace for each other,
        A Love more possible than love this world
Can offer, as the Muse does not bother,
        When a boy, I thought of you as my girl.

II

DUO

What a beautiful toast I've been humming,
Though you might not have a grave-stone up yet.
You are my love I dearly swear by,
For our world cannot end in disarray,
Since order begins like most anything
Else in the world, the milk when I'm thirsty,
My medicine which lasts beyond the grave,
For you are my life's companion, my song,
The waves of the sea, dancing tides, color,
Lapping letters ashore, ribbons of ties
White and pink, the sun, running with the blues.

What woman does love me with assurance,
The morning moving darkness drifting loose
Lively as wings silvering out of sight.
The sun's an order without shouting *rise*,
Resurrection, my soul, yours, a beauty
The world oversees, enrapt in silences
Moonshine stands erect at Attention's grave,
Design lying in churchyards needing bells
Free of clanging melody the night's sea
Wafts for color, feelings, sparkles, glitter,
Suns of Some Old Time—gods and goddesses,
Our rapture not quite extreme enough.

MOOD: FOREVER A SEQUEL

1

Now the joy we knew has cycled,
      In a tight and self-conscious brow,
            The sex and text become benumbed;
Still Hope and Time work unbuckled,
The scutcheon, Normal Mood, flayed,
      As far back as Youth its nose thumbed
At Depression's malaise—which stayed,
      A squatter we can't disavow.

2

We walked along the Fairy Glen,
      The fields, meadows, purple with wild
Layers singing for us like twins,
      The wind, singling, doubling its lyre.
The spruces blue-greened their limbs to sky,
      Where clouds accumulated and blurred,
As needles underfoot pricked dye
      A blood-red, which hurt good our words.
It was as if a floating band,
      Sent from some Elysian fields,
Played for us together to scan
      A way to Love's abundant yields.

3

We kissed among those spruces blue,
      The sky leaning on our shoulders,
Light as sunset courting the dew;
      We scraped in tunes of time, boulders,
Shadows drumming silence for us,
      Until the tree-tips stopped leaf-still,
As if to sign the wind No Fuss,
      And let the world, noiseless, reel
On the hills of Lintemarho,
      Like loaves of corridors displayed,
Arranging themselves in harmony,
      Sounding land's edge to be the sea.

4

How real it was! The quietude—
      By any other gauge The Farm
Could have been another world's rude
      Commerce centering in one form:
The feeling of too much sadness
      Folding the seasons in a row
Our eyes beheld no more than less
      A mid-summer as winter's snow:
Gingerbread men, white lake effect;
      Crab-apples, along the line-fence,
Separating neighbors, in a frieze,
      While wind whirling down chimney-stacks,
Hearthstone-bound, laughed like a giant
      And foxes, lost from all but tracks,
Loping out of grace heaven-blent;
      I did not want to pinch myself—
The trip was too rare for all show,
      An actual dream, Summer Place,
Named for sisters from Buffalo.

5

Reality's not a bad bore,
      As Shub's mind, now certainly is,
For the way that cold landscape tore
      Our hearts from ragged thoughts to bliss
Drew changes on the easel-clouds
      We cannot duplicate, our minds,
Our hearts, swinging true to limb-boughs,
      Thoughts in retrospect that seem Time's
Sword sheathed in snow a northeaster
      Might blow down our blouses to bring
Decades of grounds for bestial
      Trespasses my lines cannot sing.
Depression is a bear, I mean.
      Now I've said it—sink into
And out of any path we scheme
      Together, out of Fate's hard due.
The day's ledges cradle the hill
      In your state, making Caroline
Over and done with words to thrill
      And bring in even one spare line,
Comparisons, somber trickles
      The sand brushes in our lashes,
Closing, drawing pulley-tickles
      From wells, our souls, the fathomless
Deepened mica-bits, wide open,
      Unfocused on those laser-heights
That uncurbed mania dotes on,
      Yourself, myself, too, Nothing, blights.
Linda, Terry, Marnie, Hope—
      Lintemarho—how envious—
Welcoming the climbing, low scapes
      Storms must be—coming to lend us
What sweet recalls our eyes reveal
      Now separate in a neat scene
To dip, sway out of sync, until
      Your cycle joins the Fairy Glen.

MORE

On Paul's Hill and in Cow Mire, the butterflies land in color-kisses.
The yellow wings look like props on the piper cub I built as a boy
before I gave a kiss to the girl I thought I loved. The bushes grow

more than I can know among my shrubs and trees. August blushes
understandingly. I swing my arms in the John Deere's hum,
my clippers on my lap in case I need to cut a branch or lob the

handles to free the webs the spiders have woven since I last walked
Cow Mire Branch. I keep my body as if wired to wish a star
would jiggle through a cloud. Shadowline: faded pink. It looks

like mingles of dyes the washer happed on blend-and-sink. In
retrospect, I tear at serious-seeming touches to miss the whole
complete as what had not been torn exactly. We repeat longings

without hard breathing, lying at the end of that bed, together,
Charm and Scrub. We never say a word, yet see the light surround
in rubs of breath, places growing away from grace, sinking beauty

into spare halves to shape one soul in space and move the instant
we leave unsaid the rituals of our long embrace, joy's come-ons
every time the morning sun washes our faces. So take your pick.

Let's say that rain is good awhile for reveries; the days linger:
memories turn to powder the hay we rolled in yesterday,
without recess from quick goodbye.

LOVE CLOUDS

My song's of setting suns
That look good going down.
My only milk-cow's gone.
Please help me drive her home.
I need to press my face
Into her side again
As she eats hay and grain.

Gallons must swell the bag
Of roaming Gloria
I love now and always,
My rambling Jersey cow,
Settling in that carriage.

I hear the bucket's pings,
A milking musicale.
My freckles grace her lows.
Her tail unlays my hair.

QUIET SNOW

I am soothed by the snow turning water,
yesterdays looking like dust, varied bits
of jabber on the news; thermometers

like looking glasses when your reflection
appears, many multiple presences
of times together, when concentration

is not in the works and we speak poses
as if mentioning our names might spell joy,
our faces locking into each other's

by a storm nature creates. I bow
to you now, blowing you a kiss to woo
the fuzziness of your neck, cheeks and brows.

"Now?" you ask, knowing I am one the law
and I failed so you could lift me from *was*
for keeps and wake me up awake to know

that snow is just snow, knocking, laying its
fluffs right around as in a muffled talk
on the telephone, your lips close as light

streaks in your kitchen window. The curtain
you pull back to say, "Good morning, Morning,"
just as Mother Maytle used to open

her heart and soul to the world and then drop
a teaspoonful sugar in her Sanka,
sit by the radiator-vent and shop

for a tablecloth or spread for the bed,
humming more to herself, her *Sears* open,
not asking outside things to keep her head

up over the horrors of remembrance
of her father she thought about sure as
she was six when the mulberry did branch

when the hanging shook her; she would stand up
before the sink and glance toward the hurt.
All the snow that ever falls will not stop

her woes: in one motion her housecoat's on.
With pail in hand she runs across the road
to dob-sprinkle a cut-worm-dust-packet

into the tops of collard-leaves, way well
enough to keep worms from eating a mess
of greens smelling up the house—a bottle

of odors let loose among the quiet
snowflakes easing my mind and heart for you.
My mother glances toward me and turns out

to be you, again, after the last light
goes out in my house of dreams years ago.
Night roams astray, moving along Paul's Hill

around Sanders Road like a coyote
or deer bringing my senses to me there
at the crossing, as I remember you

asking me if I keep you in my head.
I say to myself, Yes, mumbling something
unintelligible, not good as bed,

your hand in mine before sleep completes me
to dream of respite, solid as the smell
of hog-meat cooking in collards coming

through the years out of the south, the windows
opening on the knowledge that you love
me still, as I adore you, too, without

having to say more than a nod speaks in
a way words cannot, symbol of one day
many sheets of wind blow the snowflakes all

out of proportion to consolation
or reason to rejoice that our thoughts are not
jailed in a barred-windowed space, prisoners,

that have stood at those windows looking out
on the square, whatever; I cannot well
up in my head the image which might say

the exact weight I want to say to you,
how my little Austin-Healey Sprite once
held the love day and night we two shared.

We're older-younger, the romance of
cleanliness you shine and show all that time
is never ravaged or compromised by

pride or zeal for the same colors ranging
and blinking jerseys in the sun on fields
where boys and girls team up on each other

for the perfect, indefinable One
forgiveness craves and lives for a set of
circumstances of involvement's surprise,

now, as I want to forgive myself, first,
and then, you, for keeping your head when all
about you are losing theirs for him or her.

DECADES OF PRAYER

We talk about the times to come,
You, well in my arms again: you run
Opponents ragged on the tennis court.
Your serve curves like the Shenandoah.
Your clothes whisper words
Swerving as drops
Of rain a storm brings to flaps
On Derek's Awning: rain-curtains: bird-chirps.

Hidden in forsythia my eyes
Focus: birds; it is mating season—cries
Everywhere—praise from house-finches,
The titmouse, martins and chippers,
Small sparrows, their brown caps around the oak.
The stoop guards outback where Paul's Hill lowers
Its run-off to drainage for lovers
Like us, bringing our families to the green
Meadow where the sour-mash of Cow Mire
Invites us to walk, hand in hand, side by side,
On Sunday evenings to play our hearts.

It is right the sun always wins
The contest between the sun and wind
For ceremony frees our bodies
The ebbs flow in separate selves
Coming around to be counted
For plenty, keeper of the Bounty,
Our supreme surprise Love never shelves.

Considering all, how could I be angry
At Nature's ways of sending family
Home, since we came back to my birthplace,
Here on Paul's Hill, where the meadowlark's song
Sounds like polished notes of water
Magnifying a streaming, whistling
Invitation to hear one sizzling
Spring-of-the-yeareeeee!

Though Arrogance may tighten its dance
To want the bird to say more
A dirge swells the lilac in the hedge.
The shade's dogwood and swamp-oak ledge
And lean for J.W. Pope's Angus to rest
And lounge, their tails swishing flies
Cowbirds writhe around to peck a sky
Full of stock-manure, Miracle-Gro's challenge.

Our love grows in the world's
Unhidden hedges; merry margins of giggles
Dispense laughter's squiggling screams
Setting among quarrels lost in Firewitch
Profuse as Mandevilla
Honoring feelings floundering
Stories Infinity ditches.

I want to set all evil
Aside and let Good level the bubble
That resides to shift the wind following Andrea,
Storm of fury and burn; actual
Dances, especially, waltz across enemies
Truth keeps and sets for remedies
Our feet hope for.

EMPTY SHELVES SONG

I met a girl from Pleasant Grove,
Her name's a cresting voice.
She dimpled her cheeks and wove
A web that stirred up my thirst.

After losing me she gained her tongue
And wrapped it all in pink.
Her teeth so solid white did run
Up and down our stance so sweet.

And Cow Mire Place, where she lived,
Held harmony in leaves.
She skipped down some lashing sleet
And opened her arms to me.

Now my tongue must sing
Of empty shelves my memory haunts
To brim breathlessly with dings
Electronic with occasional jaunts

To be with her who lists
With wind to sail toward my charms—
For all I need's this tall, lithe gift
To roll in my sweet baby's arms.

SIGNS OF SPRING

The days ahead
keep greening
a birding of
fluttering feathers.

In my binoculars
a scoping trophy
wheels round
on a cowbird.

The perk of dancing
redbirds at dawn:
sun-glossers, cymbals,
North Carolina's bird,

official—and you there
waiting to be hugged:
the green-black earth
March lays ready

for the nuthatches,
tree-climbers with tools,
several flinty
men jangling glints

in oak-alleys, boughs,
really, like birds
so small
in visitation, stations

dependent on spurs
sticking heavenward
with heels
climbing up and down

like one drunk and happy,
on call to chapel
to gab without
words, root a

slab of limb
a little right or left
of a crotch
where hands on chain-

saws buzz
my memory
of your white-breasted
joy calling *follow me*

as I migrate the poem
on down to Soft Nub,
the place drinking outlines
flare and thirst

never drying up.
I meditate
on the dumbfounding
treasure of spring,

no dust, just spirit
opening the steam
I saw this morning
rise up on the tin roof

of the plankhouse,
leaving me lonely
for you, the river in the trees
up over the roof,

my deepest chamber
of longing, unnuzzled,
your nostrils flared
as your face brushes

my passage and I say
It is March 10,
the purple martins
will arrive soon

and we shall be
free of winter's
exile and the cleft
of wearing-away

paths the deer shall
cross, the fox and
opossum, too, raccoon,
mostly, when I'm

not looking, as instinct
rules between us
in the shadows
where Panic undulates,

sings tenor in a
language, not mine,
though you and I, my love,
make the differences.

OUR UNSPOKEN LOVE

What have I done to keep you away?
Help me keep myself there,
Composing my reveries
To hold us on course.

The bluebird flutters,
What shall we do
To keep renewed?

Depression's care
Lingers unaware.

We could let thoughts go
Along with some friends we used to know,
Then go stir starlings from the shelter's eaves,
Their long beaks yellowing
Like lean-strung autumn beans.

The Sweet Betsy's blush prompts
The purple martin's song.
My heart upon your breasts,
My arms laced around your hips,
Your breathing I sense,
Toes, hair, lips.

MOONLIGHT

I say "roses" to you, as you swivel
your wicker chair, pose, swish your hair,
then pace up and down like one in search of
a ruse some tippling scribe might
take to bed without pretense of entanglement,
the tub I sat in long ago for my weekly bath
Romance tuned for you, since you wish
to while away your days without pain
among the low moos crunching Pope's Pasture,
a scene, rural necessity: one swain,
his love, and a cow or two, and one bull
named Shackleford. I feel like a pilgrim
whispering this, holding on, my love,
you, standing there, ready to take my hand
and turn us toward towns of memory,
places we will not have to scrounge
to find a path we can walk
without weighing thoughts or words.

Those dream-like stars turn
right into Scrooge
searching for Easter in a dream,
your rouge shaped like a dragon
designed for naked strategies trails
draw for small animals not rabid at all,
as most rabbits are ready to visit
boys and girls to lay eggs during Passion Week
in usual covenants of grain,
the farmer's green gaze and sway in wind
gone for I have taken the Scag,
cut the grass, seeing the John Deere
every time I manage a zero-turn
across the broken ground
the color of my mind,
accoutrements I cannot name.

As if nothing familiarizes bone,
I love you, your profile, too,
mine alone as you turn in my Biology class.
How I wish I could see your face
in an orchard of dreams, lobbies, backyards,
hedges lined with crabapple trees
and yarrow tufting the wind where tall pines
line Paul's Hill, plus a grand wall of banter,
baseball-talk and rue of maidens,
graves, a-mouldering;
you tell me I am your farm-boy poet,
the two of us coincidence promises.
Why? Line off our story, appropriately?

I could speak of snow, bunny slope,
a mink or two, possum, too;
then I would not think of you
set in cairn of rock-face
to state the danger around us,
the human race a cast of nerves,
scramble, enough grace,
taste of stories back to Adam,
the luster there, without a home,
candle, yet finesse, I know,
that solitary pace they took,
hunkering alone in their eyes
to bleed or bed or straighten the places
one must after the fig's torn out of mud
and poked with a lovely burning,
hot-red surmise the poet creates,
gender's lowering bar a strain on the straying
number of ducks or chicks or camels
thudding toward the ark,

waiting for word from One on high
to fix agitation's assurance
that a fuse has been lit
for necessary—good news.

        But here we are, conjunctions,
a crisis happening in our need
for an *in* on everything we hold dear,
resignation of the rose in moonlight,
the old question of crosses, persons,
maybe a dozen in the moon,
who knows, the haze in wedges
night keeps between my love
for you at dawn, my longing
when the moon sketches the lake.

        You know what I mean:
the one sweetest fact that your evasions
come to be a tact you did not try to employ,
for your head, full of sunlight,
shadows memories you have of me,
your atoning for the bed we share
in sheets of wind words lure us
toward that lonely door you open, aria,
love that never dries in the morning dew.

So why does one cry for stars before sleep
when the moon is enough to include two
who know that singing makes perfect—goodnight.

ALWAYS THERE

You are always there when I turn to munch
The past spread out like dried tufts, shriveled, cracked
Like shocks of sun-cured fodder being stacked.
Sometimes I stir the dogs that lick and scrunch
Next to me, their paws seeming to ambush
My thoughts of you, my desire to take tea
To your bedside and open up the sash
And say Look at that brightening country
Your home-place brings to bear far from the tomb
Long years ago that leaves us all awry
While Mortality gets its withered broom
And sweeps the yielding crumbs in a deadly
Rush Grief cannot prepare to upend right
When my eyes take in the finale's aim.

A voice wakens me out of the black swarm
Of bees inside my body's cells the bards
Cannot shroud or stamp as a group-party's
Worth with their volleys sliding like bloodworms
Down a line off Surf City's pier, mildew
On the posts leading to water to bid
That fields show off the coffins left to view
As unquiet souls of families you
Said one time would salute the ace of spades
Lifting from their gardens the latest news
All over the countryside that our loss
Gained a spot in love's sweet song, I suppose,
Even when you were not here and I trailed
A hurt animal obeying its call.

I turn to you all alone in my taste.
Your energy parts a road for the rood
Raising before memory leaves abrupt
Evidence that dogwood would climb a crest
Sacred as surreal motes of dust and rust.
Time washes lambs bloody as words repent
And wean themselves from use in competent

Voices wanting a bright-lasting mistrust
Of all currents flimsy for a lot of
Show in a world among baby puppies
Curling at feet of slaves whose stories seize
And reel in my heart, especially, with

The South ever rising again to lift
The past as bottom-land to be revived.
Then you appear, your face, round, plus one tear
Active below an eye, a tub of skin
In mini-bloom, standing in the smooth water
Your space, spiders gone around the molding,
Cleanliness shining on inside-out strips.
I want to pull my tools out of the rough,
Ready, displayed in hard obedience
To a falling chisel, headlong, in awe,
With clarity, aim, and understanding,
A trumpet of sounds, aloft, playing taps
And tunes calling for raps in the raking
Melody to loosen the air which shops
For care at Treasures.com, the listing
Compendium, story of you and me.

I always go mad when I see your face.
We were born to be echo's Everything—
Adaptable, forthcoming, spreading a
Trove of never-leaving energy—safe
Environment, mirror, One Somebody
Lilting and lying among reflections
Mornings until the late moon's selections
Promenade fox-fire around the barn.
I walk Cricket and see my father's stool,
His hunter's seat, quiet coves a cascade
Of dances his mind must have stored to tread
Lightly his heels he lifted in the ore-
Colored leaves of poplar Cow Mire Branch
Rivulets, waltzes, now, for you and me.

THE OLD WELL

As if breaking up could ever escape
a way your heart in Carolina blue
blurs surfaces when we dock our lightship

beside a long bus-ride to show your grace
looking backward through the years from Old East
dormitory to meet, letting your face

salvage our world anew, the replenished
fuzz Memory glimpses of UNC,
trying to focus at McCorkle Place,

for What, I ask, could stir a wilderness
the past gives to this set of symbols
around work of Eugene Lewis Harris

and return us to longing springs of this
structure, how a necessary meeting
took place, yet did not occur—confession:

I can recall my rooming in Old East
one long summer, a messy term between
my undergraduate years and now: this

Well—modeled on the Temple of Love
and lore based in the Gardens of Versailles.
The Old Well, built, 1897,

the year William Faulkner was born in New
Albany, Mississippi; benches, walls,
1954: separate-equal

was overruled. No thing more beautiful
on the campus, UNC-Chapel Hill,
for humanity's sake, a musicale,

than the people passing there—*we have drunk*—
a first draft for invisible freedom.
That's like straight A's for sure—or a slam dunk.

The Well's recognized as outstanding
architecture; that overspills hell and
above, day in, out, back to Imhotep

an architect, peacekeeper History
mourns, hushed, even though George Moses Horton
never scorned his pen—kept right on trying,

against the three-fifths-person
matter? The politicians proceeded
right on: defiance: the dorm in his name

remains the same in spring. Well's popular
first day of classes. Visual symbol
of the campus: it's photographed a lot.

If two lovers really miss each other,
wanting to see if the love they have shared
for each other could get through the bother

of time, to lather up dating and pride,
Memory joins them, walking to the Well.
The people gather round like plain sides

at feasts, with fans hoping to see athletes
sip with them from this Fountain of Good Luck,
some vandals, too, true-blue-sport rivalries.

I know a girl who gets caught in recall:
that deep bus-ride the way back to her school,
even as my mind slows myths to a crawl

for the boy, too, reports his lost Love,
the source and origin of one dark day
she wanted to know, maybe fill her cup.

LOVE SONG

I want to feel the touch of your skin.
There, your eyes and heart fix the picture
As I wish for more than I see,

When you appear in your dress
Out of the window of the second
Story of your bedroom
Over fifty years ago.

I thought you wanted to run,
Though you could not know where.
You had been put out there
To learn and lean and go on.

You instill something in me,
A thing you may be unaware of,
Glints of glances, mini-bits,
Smell and touch and sight.
Perhaps it is not to be kept,
Always freely, never complete,
Even in that moment of release.

GENTLE KISSES

I love the thought of butterflies
obstinate in air aflutter
in the sideways glance from your eyes

the way you were at first turning
the image of yourself shifting
and your love a totality
if only I could do enough
to catapult boring distance
gratitude aspires to endorse
while leaning into me the ways

your presence broadens your shoulders
when you try to pose for photos
your face, cheeks, and chin project now
in a collage of pictures
especially your lashes, too,
as you speak almost in whispers.

NIGHT AND DAY

1

You carry night, a Charm,
        Darkest spirit bright!
I dream you're in my arms—
Where all the love, your might,
Takes on the hustling Grief,
And Sadness from that Thief
        Mortality rights.

2

What joy to warp your snores?
        Lights on spangles!
I like to think you sigh more
For me than tangles
The darkness love forsakes.
An arm's length makes
        The run our Gamble!

3

Sunup's churning again.
        Foxfire haunts the meadow.
I keep coming clean,
        My love for you—your wish—
The way you make me swish
        For zestful colors.

4

Art takes on Permanence,
        Far off, not too soon,
And you tell me your cup runneth
Over—mine, too, a morn
Shining slivers of Delight
In our slight
        Chance, our bright best!

5

Ponder Death—
        Who waits for Returns?
You are my Same Breath,
My bare feet, foot-soles.

WIND-FACE

When I saw your face, your conscience
was so solid, your follicles stopped
growing and I could hear the wren inside your eyes.

In a pose the stare was starry for a man
who wanted to post your photograph, plus your coat,
for it was black like those tin-types of my great-grandfather Manly.

The girl, the woman declares,
in words nostalgia charms,
calms me down, words like "dimple," "scar," "eye."

Why are you in the taxi?
You carried your longings so long they soon
showed colors miles cannot erase.

II

The past is a drag on the lightning
swelling out its crackles and shoots in hangs
swelling inside a bedroom of thunderstorms.

So close your eyes. Let seashells
hold your oceans through funerals.
Memory plays a Dumb Show in Seawater.

Wave a rise and fall from your lifeboat.
The sail is torn; a lobe looks like a pen
of pigs on leashes for a beach-comer's eye.

To enhance faith, the past springs
its sassy moves, your street-swept
ways for joy, your girl's slip, endlessly.

We come to each other's republic,
your arms open, the woman
insisting on monitoring the girl and me.

CRASHING WAVES

This girl once I knew,
Barefooted in a dance,
Loved me and moved the rules
To wave her hands with news that's new.
Crashed the wave, what's different, a chance?

She did everything for me, plus prayed
For years while I worked; I pranced
According to routine, got regular pay
And social friends, benefits to praise.
Crashed the wave, what's different, a chance?

My employment started to peak
With snowballs and blue stockings,
Plus ice-cream of many kinds to speak
To what success smooths with official swat.
Crashed the wave, what's different, a chance?

"The poems are never done," the poet thought,
"They endorse Shub's will to rhymes."
Fools may rush to say he flourished not,
Living to write without knowing what?
And, crashing, lashed the wave, in time?

UNDER DEREK'S AWNING

As high as the hill in my boy's prayer,
I remember the yellow bus getting stuck
With mud, clay, and rain for days,
When the sky was over-blue and dandelions
Bloomed around June's edges; ticks in webs
Seized my body before the homemade,
Soaped-up wood-washtub in the pantry
Cleaned and doused me
All scrunched up in rounding bubbles
Of cloth torn from a Carolina's Best floursack.
"Shub, be sure you scrub yourself good," Mama
Would say, Titmouse sleeping nearby, my
Ears ringing *peter-peter-peter.*

The fox crossed the road without my help
And the opossum, too, though the deer had not
Yet come from the preserves the State started.
The squeals of girls and boys, the bus, leaning,
Groaning: one girl sat on a deviled egg
She left in her sack to bring home for supper,
Her family poor, the one dog, bare-boned,
The chickens more plump than family,
As they grew meat they ate, killed what they ate,
As we did.

Cricket's snug as a gnat she snaps at.
Eight chock-full inches
Of rain have fallen on Derek's Awning—
The gauge says so.

I have written these lines for you I love,
For your legs, too, and your auto-harp voice,
So lovely, yet stable as the old times
When you lifted my heart as you do now.

YOUR HEAD PILLOWED

To be first and last,
Up and down, surround, the pleasantness,
At last content like the piggy

I saw once, wiggle by my window, I, in half-sleep,
With twinges of your clear-headed knowing
You would give your heart's pulse,

You in your top of light blue leaves,
More bride than earth-angel
Up on your high bed.

You said funny things to me
To the point of my leaving and not looking
Back to see if you were looking back

To see who might be self-conscious
Or just wanting one last look
First to keep the glow that was

And then get spaced out in a maze
Of half-hearted connections
Between you and me

Until the time came when your wide-open eyes,
Two looking at me like dawn
Was ever, never going to be over, that the first

Would be the last rise waiting
Not to forget your pillowed head
And my chorus of singing tongues for you.

FOR NIN

How, my dear Nin, your body, med-ridden
(For Seroquel XR sounds like a car)
Do you adjust to drugs docs have written
For you since lithium lowered its bar
Into your being well, having smitten
Your mind's body with good and bad, a star
Hovering over the highs, while your toes
Tickle the hedges in snags of your lows;
I want to say, desiring not to bore:
My life lights up; I turn to see your face,
Especially within reach of my arms,
All of me—your chin, nose, eyes, lashes—arc
My destiny and your own woman's place,
Alone, ideal, plus our swinging alarms.

III

WALK INTO SPRING

The purple martins will come,
a scout, first,
and I shall walk

out toward the gourds,
unbeknownst to any wings
of purplish-black and those fragile,

clinging toes which look like
ink-stains among the colony.
I am home.

I distrust the starlings,
the beautiful, speckled pests,
and the house-sparrow,

especially the male,
whose badge thrusts
itself into wafting daffodils

and the pathos the phoebe
pitches and the higher landings
the eastern kingbird perches.

Somewhere "April Love"
stirs the blood of longings
and Puberty panics,

dreamy-eyed, yet composed among folklore's
lovebirds, particularly the bluebird,
over the rainbow never lifting

as I stop right
where my brimming
heels seem to put on wings.

LIFE RENEWED

The purple martin's scouting spring season,
black male of the big flock for bird-people
desiring to see gourds on poles they keep
swing gutturally dawn-songs all about
in iridescence's illumination

And sometimes the colony after frost
takes a good lover down up on his knees
with his hands checking the netting, one man;
you remember one snake the netting caught;
your skin crawls connections before a twig
tickles your pulse for the birds you alone
love on this hill, homestead; then, turning, you
wave your hand in fullness, spilled, then go on.

CLOTHES

A poet I know in a checkered coat from Belk's
Gathers an audience in a chapel in the woods
And sings songs of Don Gibson and Hank Williams,
Wearing the songs on his tongue the way two special friends
Display their hearts in strings of a violin.

      The first is dashing to and fro, nervous on the phone,
In her Söfft sandals with sexy straps and white Jennifer Lopez
Pants or some distinctly McLaughlin's long, brownish lushes
She wears at her age, getting older, she might say,
Yet beautiful in that old way love keeps desire inside.
She covers her heart that pounds and almost catches
Us together in her devilish eyes.
Her Ferragamo shoes show her ankles.
The poet thinks she might take over his muse
And make a royal salute to be most popular
Among women in her class by Customer-rating.
Still there are no softer shoes than her Ordelia's summer wedges
Or any other outer pieces I can name.
The inner? Reserved for depth-readers of *Sartor Resartus*
Or Prufrock's mirror which keeps giving back
Her friend's face, that friend who wears the same-size shoe,
Thus the Salvatore Ferragamo Women Shoes: the intimate items,
She says, have no appeal, personally, "ordinary" being the word,
Though I have felt her insides steel when at a party
She asked a woman she'd just met: "What's your husband's job?"
OB / GYN— the woman responded and that was that, the High Cotton
Clothing Store brought down to Customer Service quicker than a
Season can.

      The labeling on tops is another thing: Yansi Fugel, Doncaster,
J. McLaughlin's. I know a lady, lovely long ago as now,
Who modeled a Lady Manhattan I gave her. My sister loved these tops,
Mother, too, and this girl wore this blouse like no other
And made me feel proud to do the laundry or take it with care
Extreme to the Cleaners to be done up right and packaged for
Future wears.

Doncaster, to advance their "Fab Finds Under $250" —
Got its start, 1931, Doncaster Collar and Shirt Company,
Rutherfordton, N. C. —isn't that a musical-sounding town!
Bobo Turner, a textile-son, named the company
For a favorite honeymoon tour—Doncaster, England.
This business probably is more than you need to know
About additions: Miracle Shop, Trends, Style News,
Accessories, Essentials, Colors and Categories.

Just visit one of their outlet stores in the South.
See Ferlinghetti's "Underwear."
Hysterical, she said, or my favorite, Wilbur's
"Love Calls Us to the Things of This World."
Certainly a lot can be said of laundry, as well as the Junior League.
I know a woman who belonged there
And sang with relish, all the way, "I Fall to Pieces."
Occasionally she dabs some Chanel no. 5 behind her ears
And's energetic about red, inner and outer wear.
(Bobo backwards, by the way, is Obob.)
I can see my beloved's nose go into a puppet's clothes
Upon hearing, "My husband's an OB / GYN."

Nin, of course, looks easy and casual in any dress.
Her occasion is her destination—9 to 5—for she works
Every Essential which does not cater
To clothes for the Depressed: so she stands:
I see "Jockey" in the band, there, as she peers in her closet
For her pants and blouse to fall and put themselves
On fully voluntarily, as if a Clothes Patrol
Of trolls or little, slow-crawling Eastern Mud Turtles
Might help get her dressed: I assure you: if she had a Yansi Fugel
She would think she might blow it, sight unseen,
Or spin the top, all swirly patterned in Nutopia,
And she could not press the button, Color and Storage,
Her brain kindles—to see her wearing such possibilities.

One must make a decision first—and she cannot,
Starting inside her brain-cloudy category, wherein tees,
Tunics or tailored shirts do fail to turn her into a
J. McLaughlin woman who adores and chooses a paisley print
Or Catalina Three-quarter Sleeve Tee in Cheetah
(I am not making this stuff up) or Catalina Three-quarter
Sleeve in Python, No! And the checkered pants and Foxcroft blouse,
The chiffon? Say any of those words and she will say,
Are you talking about a cake? A boy I dated once, she'll sigh,
Drove a Catalina Pontiac. Cheetah? You mean Pita Bread?
So goes the story for today: "And remember, S. D.
On your fertilizer bag means *Square Deal*."
By the way: my name is Shelby Dean, not Smith Douglass.

FLIGHT

It was more like Ishmael in the riggings,
the way my limp
lines tended the basin

of water she used to bathe
my consciousness and then
the knot appeared and left no gain

in my groin, no grain I could feel,
though grit sanded my longings
the way acoustics go funny

in a warehouse when music's a tin-note
of color, my shadow, not-me,
more than ever, separate as the body

hovering over me, still separate, though eventually
the debt to rising
betrayal would sound its horn,

singling the troubles
doubling a rock in each hip,
rather than bones colliding and cascading

the point repose whooshes attachments
into starry, starry flights
of nights and battlefields of ants

working to get into one hole
like my mother, as a child,
crouched over a doodle-bug's home,

chanting softly, rhythmically,
come, come, get your supper
her straw of pine a motion art

teaches me through the onslaught
of years, all winds
I welcome in shouts at the top of my lungs.

THE WARMTH OF THE FIRE

In my throat sings my mind in flames.
We have gathered at the Porthole

to wallow wetness in shallows
already up to our navels,

our fingers fluttering our sleeves
and eleven curious sailors

thrashing lifeboats to take us in.
Pictures of the *Pequod* and the *Rachel*

on the wall gleam in bottle-glass.
The plastic seats for patrons crack.

Here I am, looking for my craft.
The storm which stained our raft

decades ago's a berry-haw,
calm as stuff which settles in thaws.

You serve a hot roast you have baked,
Then cut us each some carrot-cake.

SEARCHING

I walk among the streams and ferns of Cow Mire. Sour-mash, partridge-berry, dogwood, and goose-grass gather the hermit thrush out of the red clay Rose loves.

Sun eases out to her in Morningside Assisted Living. Squirrels seem happy; the wren scolds me, my posture a threat to its nesting box beside the terrace.

August is spider month. Ticks lounge in webs. Rains have fallen on the wild cat and the old litard-stump, the haw of old-timey fence-post fame, the berries almost not-red around the path under the tulip-poplars.

Branches run and meet, if enough rain falls. I see your face everywhere I turn. I cannot quite touch you. You are the rooster's crow, tractor's hum, breeze blowing outward here—promoting the pale light the hawthorn keeps, that small breath of green so quiet, after the rains. Doves jet-stream over Paul's Hill.

LOVE REMEMBERED

My father's hands, like oiled, softened mitts
from his sandlot baseball days, move over my mother's
arms like home runs without pitches to guide
the fifty-eight years of their marriage,
the rage of cancer all over him, except his eyes
fixed in *his* mother's bluing squinches.
He says one more time, "My heels are long as pine-cones"—
his sockless feet in dried, old-man, bean-looking
slabs on the rented bed of his display
before Rose & Graham Funeral Home
sends their men to come
and get him.
It is not a Valentine's Day,
as today, but the fall of the year,
a definite withdrawing, beside the mark,
where, as "Master," he no longer
can be: father, baseball player, checker-champ,
fox-hunter, horn-blower, dog-lover,
cigar-smoker (White Owls), Stetson-hat wearer,
somebody, he would say, the girls thought, when he would enter a room.

Above his brows the whitening forehead under the black hair,
his girls all around, the lithe one, with the hair
of swish and the smile in the voice
readying for the slide of wish and browse
for the good man, hard to find, the parent,
the weathering sense of plunging onward
toward a drought after which Heaven
smokes up the morning fields
where his dogs gather to smell the past
on the wind which blows right once
for the race to run itself in the sweetbriars
of youth, when he would grin a rabbit to a box
he threw together like some backwoods
Prospero out to design a bubble
for the sex-slush of come-on and lather,
then stand before the mirror in the bathroom,

shaving and mumbling to himself while his Maytle,
my mother, gets breakfast and puts it
on the table in front of him, his coffee
a purgatory black enough to strengthen
the trembling breaths of bear in the magazines
on hunting he reads, his hunting pants, Ball Band Boots,
his shells, shotgun, rifle, the baby-basket
strung with light blue ribbon atop the chifferobe
in the middle-room in front of the slop jar.

He is gone in no time.
I walk through the three rooms of the plankhouse.
He is everywhere, the lantern we used possum-hunting
on a nail by the pantry: *the sun goes down
and I am lonesome and sad, lonesome and sad,*
wondering what am I going to do. When I go
to his grave I feel the sun's stung-glow
around my ears. It is a perfect Sunday
evening and the cocked bluebird's eye
dabs detail of spring behind my ears.
Clear-eyed, I know the power of love.
I have no pad to say in words: later, I think—
thirty-five years sooner than farther down the road.

Now the praise of women brings sorrow
odd as a parting embrace
which puts the icing on an unmade cake
and brings a heart-song to mind—"romance,"
a word now, one marriage sequesters.

THE MOTHER'S TALE

I walked away from the plot she sure-god
Did not prepare for anything she'd plant,
Her memory leaving her so she could
Not get up herself, flat in Sunnybrook,
A name she would approve, since she believed
Every hyped word in her *Southern Living*.
I could hear her voice, standing at the sink.

"I reckon this kitchen's been good to me,
And life, too, since I've cut crinkly patterns
Out for dresses for me and Maytle Rose
And you boys: I made your shirts, darned your socks.
I've kept my Paul happy, too, I reckon.
I told him—would be something else to spend
Half his dog-money on his family.
Mama thought I was much too young to court.
I was sweet sixteen; Paul would walk the road
From Paul's Hill three miles to St. Mary's Grove
To see me, and Mama said he stayed here
So much we might as well go and marry,
Raise a family, start a little farm.
He always said I could do a man's work.
In the fall I would put the dried field-peas
In a washed guano sack, take a stick
And thrash it across like it was bubbling.
I'd put the peas in a pail, find the wind;
Real slow, empt my bucket in another.
Mama would tell me—*Go winnow the peas*.
Hogkilling time I could thread a hog's gut
With a peachtree limb good as anything
You've ever seen and turn each intestine,
Stripping the offal to get the casings
Ready to stuff the homemade link-sausage.
Paul loved chittlins like he loved coconut
Or me: when we started out he called me
Dumpling. Like the song, I was five foot two."

FLOWERS IN THE SNOW

I

I crunched. Prints. Snow's aftermath—
I was among Rufous-sided Towhees and the tremors
from the wings of redbirds at the squirrel-proof feeder,
the green bar, downward, slicing forsythia

intimately enough to send up my body heat.
I had three more feeders to fill: one in the hush
of the leaning basketball post, another under the chainey,
and one in the little red house, wild birdseed,

its chimney a roof to top off the slant
the juncos and finches, like flashing neons
as Cardinals alight, fluttering
patterns tenderness encourages

in pearls of red: I wonder where
the bluebirds go in this weather, no insects
for them to chase in their didos.
I must make a mixture for them:

render some beef fat into suet,
together with a cup of peanut butter
and yellow corn meal: I'll dream for them
some of Mr. Jack Finch's meal worms,

and his special dogwood berries, too,
until I hear the bluebirds and see flashing
their colors in my food for them,
until they come home from this storm,

its secret come up from the south to speak
no more about birds trapped inside my
longing for a girl I have known half a century,
her prayer, mine, for better flurries.

I know her name I hardly speak,
for beating wings happen in a litany
I cannot tell, the draught of words
blowing up the chimney in a fire I built

for the two of us this morning,
the sun not out, the dry-snowy
air fed by the rush of ring-feathers
flitting around these four feeders.

II

Blurred swelterings I saw yesterday, the quince
flushing and crossing its boughs,
little sweaters of snow like stoles and cords

among bare limbs the February cold polishes
as if expecting my Bean boots to turn into
mini-kayaks plowing linens of liquid

shaking the birds in patches the years
turn in the name of an old
bicycle I owned and sold to Percy Bolling

for five dollars, I believe, to ride out
this prose: I think it was a Rambler.
Judging from the many cardinals, mostly male,

I'm pretty sure the bike was blue.
My arms open wide for the birds, their show
about to start: I'll wait for pre-dark for the red

to publish the grounding white; for now the tufted
titmouse, house-finch, white-throated sparrow,
the chickadee, wren, the jo-reet, my father said,

the dove sitting on the hillock up from the feeder,
the territory whole as the territorial one,
Mr. Mockingbird, struts and flits

a jackknife of feathers my looks
tame toward the evening's drizzle
when the six o'clock newsmen and women

post a photo of a redbird in the snow,
and, with cameras rolling, visit the highways of ice.

DRIZZLE

My face marbled with mist.
Goddesses stored stones in rolls around my head.

The sun dished the sheets.
I cupped my hands; my fingers sang in my skin's band.

A blankness came over me, passion's fashion.
Showers lined unpredictability as mission.

Slanting sideways my cheeks, I felt rivulets in a ruckus.
I wanted to hold my guitar, longing to rush on stage like opry-stars.

The sleet became slushy; the hail of my years rained.
I could feel cold, wet, soggy pounces of Diana's diamonds

Plinking my face, needles changing to rosebuds, breasts, kiss-bumps,
Then to little poplar blossoms most-pleasurable, regulating space, reward,

My sky's blanket, wrapped, as if to say—*slate*.
No cloth I had to wash my tears in aftertaste.

STORMS NEVER LAST

The morning after scatters.
The lawn's a litter of sticks:
Pick up poplar, oak, maple, mostly,
Haul them off to Cow Mire Branch.

NOTE TO DIANA

Thank you for your Ode,
The cadence you bring in words
Without closing out the world around,

What in and out the same
Oneness we aspire, the wonder
Around every instant of seconds

Coming and going even now
As December almost grins in sun
Shining on the grass outside
My window, just to show us how

To write a poem, sing a song,
Love one another, even as
Night sequesters mortality

And comes on to light
High and low and in between
Grace and humility you name.

STASH

Swish-face, straight-hair, bloom of the crest,
Tall-pixie, little budding-dish:
Where did you come from—the west?
Out of a grove—a princess?
And now, your secrets in the shrine
You call a "stash," a dash of this and that:
Handkerchiefs from Croatia,
Some basic, sun-struck whispers
Of love's space, a lot of love in place of
Yourself opening a door, your feet on the floor
Shuffling, "come on in."
I am like a reed inside your den
Noise cannot conquer: *secrets*, the weeping
Inside to keep my eyes open to your sleeping.

A stream of neighbors answers your keeping,
Your trail of steps making them
Happy in your singularity; still
You keep your eyes out for me, your farm
Boy from childhood I know, Purgatory,
Gateway to Research Triangle's air:
I throw open the sash for longing and poetry
Until the fig-leaf turns into a star.
I keep you as the flower you are, a rose
Today, a fern tomorrow when we'll walk among grain
To Cow Mire which will receive our hoes
Once we enter the path at the ash; the long virgin
Stand of pine, the one sour-mash, the poplar-feasts,
The sassy way the stash represents your breasts,

As if I kneel at the brink of your keyhole,
After all the years turn and open
The door to your breath and your sweet confessional
Until that day in March I saw your honey-skinned,
Broad shoulders, a meadow across your back
Through that hole, mind you, your dress

A wrap, red, the window facing my south of luck
Opening cotton-fields of your kindness
As little pallets of children play and rout
Out the autumn sunshine with their open
Baby-talk and fingers touching sunlight.
I retrieve my past into your powers.
My heart rushes like an old self set free,
Transformed, a *just-is-thing*, under a big oak tree.

LAMENT

I love you more to venture that I love
        Midst trouble and fatigue; yet I know not
An alternative to quicken our peace
        Intensified by state of health and lack
Of Fortune's blooming zest—
Embraces, warm charms—divine—
        The flowering stars—bone-blossoming breast—
And soul—as you give all,
To live for mornings after night's falling
        Truth, separation's misery, silence.

DEAREST

The day the night lets alone
For morning's steadying picture
Darkness glimpses while letting go.

LITTLE FARM DOGS

Like a necessary lover I survey the land
laid out like a pattern, seeing again
my mother preparing to give her hand

to sewing, humming as she cuts a line
with her scissors squeaking beside
images of two Norwich Terriers whose burden

for me salvages our straight-ahead ride
life turns to a lovely lush,
presence of activity all day—and then to bed,

precisely as instinct governs dogs off leash,
first Long Valley Jamie that loved the stars
as he lit my life for almost two decades, a rush

plentifully edgy toward me the way lovers
belong to one another to set
relationships in definite surrounds like quivers

nestling unused in a pouch: Cricket roves
in my shadow, never seeming to leave
my side. She's fifteen now, never bereft of moves.

Jamie lived to be almost eighteen, his essence
during those years more than any rite
out of nature I recall from my own presence

as a farm-boy here on Paul's Hill, the sight
of small game like opossum, quail, rabbits, the paw-dust
of raccoon and prowls at night

in my dreams of animals crawling across my chest,
light-headed from loss of logs and loyalty
to the real thing. I am in earnest

to be ready for the rush and dashes
and then to awake and forget,
happy to be available to love's flashes.

It is as if the freedom of feet races
along on nothing more than bone,
my own, with some raindrops falling grace

and tone, heard without nightmare or tears
going and coming in on me to speak
a language little farm dogs form in choirs

to rehearse, breathe, and snore without rage
that reality I underscore, as the Norwich's hearty
manner roots its journey in an image

life cannot lose, yet sends instinct through seem
until no tangent exists to oppose the rampant
circling and spilling above the brim

an energy gleaming as I tell them,
the dogs, I mean, to have some sympathy
for mirrorment: the cloudbursts

drive Cricket crazy; why, she shakes like a bee
all fuzzed-up and dying to look at
the sunshine again to run thickly,

as she is bred to do—in downpours: it's her way of talking.

SONGBIRDS

I heard new songs sung for me
at the four feeders in the yard
here at Paul's Hill,

tuned the ruffling feathers
of the towhee and watched
the sun soak the mink-breasted

female cardinal alone
in the forsythia, with three lit-red
bulbs, Christmas in early March,

the quince quivering crystal
deep, the tail-end of
what, I hope, is the last winter storm.

If I could choose one
bird to lead the intoners
and dibble their choir's enclosure

near me, I'd choose them
all, each and every one,
for scheming's not my thing

today: rufous-sided towhee,
dove, goldfinch, redbird, white-throated
sparrow, chipping sparrow, house

sparrow, titmouse, wren, chickadee,
hairy woodpecker, cowbird, and, oh, once,
the bluebird that does not make

history at the feeders: the one
red-winged blackbird's allegiance,
emptying its cough-call, I especially like.

POEM

Love, let's care for children we never had.
You know how *it* is, detours, muddy rows,
The falling for someone new who helped make
A life for you in your taste for bright clothes.

Red is your favorite color, still is,
With the botching symbolism attached.
Your nightgown, too: I do not want to miss.
It remains the clothing you relax in.

Now falling leaves, Octobering our years,
We shall love more, adoring Samantha.
That is my mother's middle name, the clear
Sweet rhyme which rings that she was a banker.

She put money aside she made from work—
Subscriptions **Herald** marked a Mason jar
She buried with a broken spade for luck.
Her children love her; everyone's a star.

COUNTERING TERMINUS

I

When I picked her up, I would say
Hello among the smell of brakes.

She was always waiting without
Benefit of wanting closed doors.

I hear a bus's engine now
And listen for her eyelashes.

It is no wonder I expect
Her to appear, here, as she will.

II

I prefer purple martin's glow
To the Bradford Exchange's shout—

"Our Forever Love Diamond Ring."
They say—"Limited Quantities."

She lays down a dream-drain my mouth
Suffers no stoppage of run-off.

III

No one can own a piece of land.
I'm growing up with that knowledge.

The graves flourish at Rehobeth,
Just as they are, without a plan.

Without one plea I know the briars
Shoot vines and they are not my own,

So long as I party without
Parleying out all the good times.

SLIPS IN THE NIGHT

Or ships, as I think of you, saying things
like that, the figure another mixture
necessarily not brews I never
quaffed: so I turn the cup up as you pass
in your *Longfellow* my *Whitman*, hoping
not to torpedo wallows of meadows
for chance at vision busing a shroud of
Shadowline where you stand still in your gown.

RUNNING TOWARD HAIR

As I came through Chapel Hill,
I wanted to run my fingers through your hair.
You went to bed in the widow's home instead
After Bacchus wined you good
And left me in the cold with one strand
Caught in a lover's glance.

Your mother and father were in another state.
You could have fallen in love with the widow's house!
Yet morning came and I arrived for you.
Your hair was straight as Poverty, innate, astir,
With streaks of wetness—a vulnerable blur.
I could tell you were caught in a lover's glance.

All girls are not caught up the same.
I know one whose hair's really curly.
Still she just as well sleep in a widow's house.
She stands for hours in front of the looking-glass
And shushes her hair with spread fingers, as if that
Might aid my seeing her in a lover's glance.

I love the sighs as you dry your hair on my shoulder
And bind the moment in the mirror with those fine
Brush strokes you swish for your lover's glance.

FLUMMOXED & BUMFUZZLED

When I am not with you I hear people say
Where is she who sings with you
And I look aside and another so lovely appears,
Two images which shift back and forth
And one brings me orange slices on a plate
And I want to call my mother.

ANXIETY

Our love's a flutter
The butterfly stutters.

Shelby Stephenson is Poet Laureate of North Carolina. His recent books are *Paul's Hill: Homage to Whitman* (Sir Walter Press); *Elegies for Small Game* (Press 53), winner of Roanoke-Chowan Award; *Fiddledeedee* (reissue, Press 53); *Family Matters: Homage to July, the Slave Girl* (Bellday Books), winner of the Bellday Prize; *Maytle's World* (play). He is recipient of the Distinguished Alumnus Achievement Award, 2015, Department of English, University of Wisconsin-Madison, and is Professor Emeritus, University of North Carolina-Pembroke, where he served as editor of *Pembroke Magazine* from 1979 until his retirement in 2010. He lives at the homeplace on Paul's Hill, where he was born, near McGee's Crossroads, about ten miles northwest of Benson.

www.ingramcontent.com/pod-product-compliance
Lightning Source LLC
LaVergne TN
LVHW041342080426
835512LV00006B/577